WORKBOOK FOR THE

WORLD CENTRAL

KITCHEN COOKBOOK

A TRANSFORMATIVE GUIDE TO

FEEDING HUMANITY, FEEDING

HOPE

BY

SAMUEL BRADFORD

INTRODUCTION

Welcome to a transformative journey through the pages of "The World Central Kitchen Cookbook" workbook. Within these digital pages, you're about to embark on an exploration that transcends the culinary world, delving into the heart and soul of humanitarian efforts, compassion, and the incredible impact of food.

This workbook serves as your guide, your companion, and your source of inspiration. It is a testament to the enduring belief that food has the power not only to nourish bodies but also to feed hope, ignite change, and unite communities. As you delve into its depths, prepare to be immersed in the stories, values, and recipes that define the World Central Kitchen's mission.

The World Central Kitchen: Feeding Humanity, Feeding Hope

At its core, "The World Central Kitchen Cookbook" is a celebration of dignity and perseverance. Its primary text, authored by José Andrés, World Central Kitchen, and Sam Chapple-Sokol, takes you on a captivating journey through the organization's origins, its tireless work, and its unwavering commitment to providing immediate food relief to communities impacted by natural disasters and humanitarian crises.

The cookbook features an array of recipes inspired by the many places World Central Kitchen has served, intertwined with inspiring narratives from the chefs and volunteers who stand on the front lines. The pages are adorned with photographs capturing moments of community and hope, and stunning food photography showcasing mouthwatering recipes.

Navigating the Workbook

Now, in this workbook, we take you even deeper into the heart of World Central Kitchen's mission. This supplementary guide doesn't just reiterate what the main book covers; it invites you to become an active participant in the journey. Over the course of four immersive weeks, we will explore the themes, values, and recipes that define WCK.

You will be welcomed into the world of food as a force for good, guided through exercises, questions, action plans, and affirmations, all designed to help you internalize the profound lessons that World Central Kitchen imparts. Each week is a new chapter in your own culinary adventure, filled with opportunities to reflect, learn, and make a difference.

WEEK 1

"INSPIRATION AND MISSION"

Welcome to Week 1 of "The World Central Kitchen Cookbook" workbook, where we embark on a remarkable journey into the heart and soul of World

9

Central Kitchen (WCK). This week is your gateway to understanding the inspiration and mission that drive this extraordinary organization, making you an integral part of the humanitarian effort to feed humanity and foster hope.

As you delve into this week's activities, you'll be drawn into the world of WCK, a place where culinary expertise meets unwavering compassion. Let's begin by exploring the core of this incredible mission.

Introduction to World Central Kitchen (WCK)

Picture yourself standing at the threshold of a global movement that harnesses the power of food to bring relief, healing, and hope to communities in need. This is the essence of World Central Kitchen, an organization founded by the visionary chef, José Andrés, and his dedicated team.

WCK is not just an organization; it's a force of goodwill, a symbol of culinary excellence with a purpose. Throughout this week, you'll uncover the roots of WCK, learn how it all began, and gain insight into the dynamic spirit that fuels its initiatives. You'll discover the remarkable journey of José Andrés, the man whose culinary prowess and humanitarian heart brought WCK into existence.

The Mission and Values of WCK

Now, let's dive deeper into the core principles that guide WCK. At the heart of this organization are values that transcend borders and unite people from all walks of life. Through compelling narratives and heartfelt accounts, you'll gain a profound understanding of the values that drive WCK's tireless efforts. These values include empathy, resilience, community, and above all, the belief that food is a universal language of love and healing.

By the end of this section, you'll not only appreciate the significance of these values but also understand how they shape WCK's mission to provide immediate food relief in the face of disasters and crises worldwide.

Stories of Chefs and Volunteers on the Front Lines

Prepare to be inspired by the real heroes behind World Central Kitchen. Throughout this week, you'll hear the voices and stories of the chefs and volunteers who stand on the front lines, ready to make a difference when disaster strikes. These are the individuals who selflessly dedicate their time and culinary skills to serve those in need, often in the most challenging and perilous conditions.

Their accounts will take you on a journey to disaster zones, where hope emerges amidst chaos, and where the power of a warm meal can provide solace to those who have lost everything. These stories will serve as a testament to the resilience of the human spirit and the boundless potential for kindness.

Foreword by Stephen Colbert

As you approach the culmination of this week's exploration, you'll be treated to a special insight from Stephen Colbert. His foreword to "The World Central Kitchen Cookbook" encapsulates the essence of the cookbook and the mission it represents. Through his words, you'll gain a deeper understanding of why this cookbook is not just a collection of recipes but a celebration of humanity, dignity, and perseverance.

By the end of this week, you will have taken the first steps in understanding the driving force behind World Central Kitchen. You'll be inspired by the stories, motivated by the values, and enlightened by the mission that unites a global community of chefs, volunteers, and supporters.

EXERCISES

1. **Reflecting on Values**: Take some time to reflect on the values of empathy, resilience, and community. Write down how you can incorporate these values into your daily life.

2. **Your Culinary Journey**: Share a personal culinary memory or experience that has had a meaningful impact on your life. Consider how food can bring people together.

3. **Acts of Kindness**: Challenge yourself to perform a small

act of kindness for someone in your community. Document the experience and its impact.

4. **Mapping Your Mission**: Imagine you're starting your own charitable organization. What would its mission and values be? Describe your vision for making a positive impact.

5. **Culinary Compassion**: Try cooking a meal for someone in need, whether it's a friend, family member, or a local

shelter. Share your experience and the recipe you chose.

QUESTIONS

1. What aspect of WCK's mission resonates with you the most, and why?

2. How do you think the combination of culinary expertise and humanitarian work can create positive change in the world?

3. In what ways can you contribute to your local community, drawing inspiration from the values of WCK?

4. What do you think motivates chefs and volunteers to work on the front lines in disaster zones?

5. After reading Stephen Colbert's foreword, what emotions or thoughts does the mission of WCK evoke in you?

ACTION PLANS

1. **Volunteer Opportunities**: Research local volunteer opportunities in your community and identify one that aligns with the values of WCK. Plan to get involved.

2. **Supporting WCK**: Explore ways to support WCK's emergency response efforts, such as fundraising or spreading awareness on social media. Set a timeline for your involvement.

23

3. **Culinary Learning**: Commit to learning a new culinary skill or recipe that you can share with others. Set a goal for when you'll master it.

4. **Community Building**: Identify a community project or event in your area that promotes unity and resilience. Make a plan to participate or contribute.

5. **Values Integration**: Select one of the values discussed this week (empathy, resilience, or community) and incorporate

it into your daily life. Document your progress and experiences.

AFFIRMATIONS

1. I am inspired by the mission of WCK, and I believe in the power of food to heal and bring people together.

2. I am committed to embodying the values of empathy, resilience, and community in all aspects of my life.

3. I recognize that small acts of kindness can create a ripple effect of positive change in my community.

4. I have the ability to make a meaningful impact through culinary compassion and volunteer work.

5. I am part of a global community that shares the belief in the dignity of all and the importance of building longer tables, not higher walls.

WEEK 2

"RECIPES FROM DISASTER ZONES"

Welcome to Week 2 of "The World Central Kitchen Cookbook" workbook. This week is a culinary exploration that will transport you to the heart of disaster-stricken areas, where the value of "Urgency" takes center stage. Get ready to immerse yourself in the world of recipes born out of necessity, resilience, and a desire to provide quick and portable nourishment to those in need.

Recipes Inspired by Disaster-Stricken Areas

As you journey through this week, you'll discover a unique

aspect of World Central Kitchen's culinary mission. The recipes featured here are not just about taste; they are a testament to the incredible ability of food to bring comfort and hope even in the most dire circumstances.

Imagine the scenes in disaster-stricken areas, where the simple act of sharing a meal can provide solace and strength. These recipes are the result of chefs and volunteers working tirelessly to provide immediate relief to communities facing unimaginable challenges. They represent the embodiment of WCK's commitment to addressing the urgency of hunger in times of crisis.

Highlighting the Value of "Urgency"

The value of "Urgency" is a driving force behind World Central Kitchen's work. It signifies the swift response and dedication to ensuring that no one goes hungry when disaster strikes. In this section, you'll delve deep into what "Urgency" means in the context of WCK's mission.

You'll gain insight into the meticulous planning and rapid deployment of resources that allow WCK to be on the ground serving meals within hours of a disaster. The urgency of their response is a lifeline to those in desperate need, and it's a value that sets WCK apart in the world of humanitarian relief.

Lahmajoun Flatbread from Beirut

One of the culinary gems that you'll explore this week is the Lahmajoun Flatbread, a recipe inspired by the devastating explosion that rocked Beirut in 2020. This dish is more than just a combination of ingredients; it's a symbol of resilience and hope in the face of tragedy.

Through detailed instructions and personal anecdotes, you'll learn how to prepare this flavorful and portable meal that was instrumental in providing nourishment to the affected communities. The Lahmajoun Flatbread is a testament to the power of food to heal and unite, even in the darkest of times.

Other Quick and Portable Dishes

Beyond the Lahmajoun Flatbread, this week will introduce you to a diverse array of quick and portable dishes that have played crucial roles in WCK's relief efforts. From soups and sandwiches to energy-packed snacks, you'll discover the art of creating meals that can be enjoyed on the go.

These recipes are not only delicious but also practical, designed to meet the urgent nutritional needs of disaster survivors and first responders.

As you explore these dishes, you'll gain an appreciation for the creativity and resourcefulness of chefs and volunteers who adapt their culinary skills to address the most pressing of situations.

By the end of this week, you'll not only have a deeper understanding of the role of food in disaster relief but also a collection of recipes that you can use to make a positive impact in your own community or share with those in need.

EXERCISES

1. **Cooking for Urgency**: Select one of the quick and portable recipes introduced this week and prepare it in your own kitchen. Reflect on the experience and consider how this type of meal could make a difference in an urgent situation.

2. **Emergency Preparedness**: Research emergency preparedness measures in your area. Create a list of essential food items that are easy to store and prepare in case of a disaster. Share this information with your friends and family.

3. **Sharing Stories**: Reach out to a local community organization or shelter and inquire about their experiences with food relief efforts during emergencies.

37

Share their stories and insights with others to raise awareness of the importance of such initiatives.

4. **Cooking for a Cause**: Plan a small gathering or event where you prepare quick and portable dishes inspired by this week's recipes. Invite friends and family to join, and consider donating the proceeds or meals to a local charity or disaster relief organization.

5. **Recipe Innovation**: Challenge yourself to create a new quick and portable recipe that is both nutritious and delicious. Experiment with ingredients and preparation methods, and document your process and the final result.

QUESTIONS

1. What are some key challenges in providing food relief in

disaster-stricken areas, and how does WCK address them with a sense of urgency?

2. How can quick and portable meals play a crucial role in providing nourishment and comfort to those affected by disasters?

3. In what ways can individuals and communities contribute to addressing the urgent food needs of disaster survivors, even without formal organizations like WCK?

4. Reflecting on the Lahmajoun Flatbread recipe, what emotions or symbols does this dish carry, and how does it connect to the value of "Urgency"?

5. What inspires you most about the resourcefulness and creativity of chefs and volunteers who adapt their culinary skills to meet urgent needs?

ACTION PLANS

1. **Emergency Food Kit**: Create an emergency food kit with the essential items you identified in Exercise 2. Store it in a designated place in your home, and make sure your family is aware of its location.

2. **Local Support**: Reach out to a local disaster relief organization or food bank and inquire about volunteer

opportunities. Commit to volunteering during a disaster response training or event.

3. **Community Cooking**: Organize a cooking workshop or demonstration in your community to teach others how to prepare quick and portable meals. Share the recipes you've learned from this week.

4. **Recipe Sharing**: Compile a collection of quick and portable recipes and distribute it to friends, family,

or your local community. Include information on their nutritional value and storage tips.

5. **Emergency Contacts**: Create a list of emergency contacts and resources in your area, including local shelters and organizations that provide food relief. Share this list with your loved ones and neighbors.

AFFIRMATIONS

1. I recognize the importance of urgency in addressing food needs during emergencies and am committed to supporting relief efforts in my community.

2. I believe in the power of quick and portable meals to provide nourishment and comfort to those facing adversity.

3. I am inspired by the resilience of communities in disaster-

stricken areas and their ability to find hope through food.

4. I acknowledge the creativity and resourcefulness of chefs and volunteers who make a difference through culinary expertise.

5. I am part of a global community that understands the value of providing immediate food relief in times of   crisis.

WEEK 3

"NOURISHING HOPE"

Welcome to Week 3 of "The World Central Kitchen Cookbook" workbook, a week that brings you to the heart of culinary compassion and the transformative power of food.

This week is an exploration of recipes that do more than nourish; they bring comfort and hope to those facing unimaginable challenges. Get ready to embark on a journey that highlights the value of "Hope" and reveals the extraordinary capacity of food to inspire resilience.

Recipes that Bring Comfort and Hope

As you immerse yourself in the

pages of this week, you'll encounter a collection of recipes carefully crafted to provide not only sustenance but also solace. These are dishes that have been prepared with love and empathy, knowing that a warm meal can be a source of strength and inspiration during trying times.

These recipes go beyond the ordinary; they are culinary expressions of hope, designed to lift spirits and bring a sense of normalcy to those experiencing crises. Each dish tells a story of resilience and the indomitable human spirit.

Highlighting the Value of "Hope"

In this section, you'll delve into the value of "Hope" and its profound significance in the work of World Central Kitchen. Hope is a guiding light in the darkest of times, a belief in better days ahead, and a source of unwavering determination.

Through the stories shared in this week's activities, you'll witness how hope becomes a driving force for both the volunteers who prepare these meals and the individuals and families who receive them. The power of hope is evident in every recipe, every act of service, and every moment of connection.

Ukrainian Borsch for Families in Crisis

One of the culinary masterpieces that you'll explore this week is Ukrainian Borsch, a dish that carries with it the resilience of a nation enduring unimaginable challenges. This recipe is more than just a combination of ingredients; it's a symbol of a people's determination to find hope in the face of adversity. Through detailed instructions and personal anecdotes, you'll learn how to prepare this hearty and comforting meal that has provided solace to families living through an unthinkable invasion. The Ukrainian Borsch represents the ability of food to nourish not only the body but also the spirit, fostering a sense of unity and hope in the midst of turmoil.

Chicken Chili Verde for California Firefighters

Another remarkable recipe featured this week is Chicken

Chili Verde, a dish prepared with deep gratitude for the brave firefighters who battle wildfires in California. This recipe embodies the spirit of community and support, as chefs and volunteers come together to provide nourishment to those on the front lines.

You'll discover the secrets behind crafting this flavorful and heartwarming dish, understanding how it serves as a symbol of appreciation and hope for the firefighters who put their lives on the line. Chicken Chili Verde is a reminder that food has the power to uplift and unite, even in the face of the most challenging circumstances.

By the end of this week, you'll not only appreciate the role of food in providing comfort and hope but also gain a collection of recipes that carry with them the essence of resilience and the enduring power of the human spirit.

EXERCISES

1. **Cooking for Comfort**: Select one of the comforting recipes introduced this week and prepare it in your own kitchen. Reflect on the experience and consider how this type of meal can bring comfort to those facing adversity.

2. **Spreading Hope**: Research local charitable organizations

or community groups that provide meals to individuals and families in crisis. Volunteer your time to help prepare and serve meals to those in need.

3. **Storytelling through Food**: Share a personal story of how food has brought hope and comfort to your life or the lives of others. Reflect on the emotions and connections that food can create.

4. **Supporting Local Heroes**: Identify local first responders

or healthcare workers who could benefit from a homemade meal. Prepare a dish from this week's recipes and deliver it to them as a gesture of appreciation.

5. **Recipe for Resilience**: Create a new recipe inspired by the concept of hope and resilience. Imagine the ingredients and flavors that would embody these qualities and share your recipe with friends and family.

1. **QUESTIONS**

   How does the value of "Hope" play a role in the work of World Central Kitchen, both for volunteers and the communities they serve?

2. What is the significance of comfort food in times of crisis, and how does it impact the emotional well-being of individuals and families?

3. In what ways can individuals and communities provide comfort and hope to those

facing adversity, beyond sharing meals?

4. Reflecting on the Ukrainian Borsch recipe, how can a dish become a symbol of resilience and unity during challenging times?

5. What do you find most inspiring about the dedication of chefs and volunteers who prepare meals with the intention of bringing hope to others?

ACTION PLANS

1. **Cooking for Others**: Commit to preparing a comforting meal for someone in your community who is facing a difficult time. Document your experience and the impact it has on the recipient.

2. **Supporting Local Initiatives**: Research local organizations or initiatives that provide food relief to those in need. Make a plan to donate or

volunteer your time and resources.

3. **Recipe Sharing**: Organize a recipe-sharing event with friends or family, focusing on dishes that bring comfort and hope. Encourage each participant to prepare and share their chosen recipe.

4. **Acts of Kindness**: Challenge yourself to perform five acts of kindness throughout the week, whether it's helping a neighbor, sending an uplifting

message, or preparing a meal for someone in need.

5. **Culinary Connection**: Reach out to a family member or friend you haven't spoken to in a while and invite them to a virtual cooking session. Prepare a comforting recipe together and reconnect through food.

AFFIRMATIONS

1. I believe in the power of food to provide comfort and hope

to those facing adversity, and I am committed to sharing this nourishing spirit with others.

2. I recognize that hope is a driving force that can inspire resilience and determination in the face of challenges.

3. I am inspired by the stories of chefs and volunteers who use their culinary expertise to make a positive impact on the lives of others.

4. I acknowledge the significance of comfort food in bringing

solace and emotional well-being to individuals and communities.

5. I am part of a global community that understands the healing power of food and its ability to foster hope and unity.

WEEK 4

"CELEBRITY SUPPORT AND BEYOND"

Welcome to the inspiring and final week of "The World Central Kitchen Cookbook" workbook. This week, we embark on a journey filled with celebrity support and the far-reaching impact of those who have lent their names and culinary talents to the cause of feeding humanity and feeding hope. Get ready to explore recipes from famous WCK supporters and discover how their contributions go beyond the kitchen, leaving a lasting imprint on the world.

Recipes from Famous WCK Supporters

As we delve into the pages of this week, you'll be introduced to a remarkable aspect of World Central Kitchen's mission — the support and collaboration of renowned celebrities and chefs. These individuals have joined hands with WCK, not just as names on a list, but as passionate advocates for the power of food to change lives.

Each recipe featured in this section represents a unique culinary perspective, a testament to the diverse and talented community that supports WCK's humanitarian efforts. These are dishes prepared with love, with the knowledge that they carry the hopes and dreams of those who believe in WCK's mission.

Breakfast Tacos by Michelle Obama

One of the culinary treasures you'll explore this week is Breakfast Tacos by none other than Michelle Obama. These tacos go beyond being a delicious breakfast; they represent a commitment to nourishing both body and mind. With Michelle Obama's dedication to health and well-being, these tacos are not just a recipe; they are a message of hope, encouraging us to start our day with nourishing choices.

You'll discover the secrets behind crafting these flavorful and wholesome tacos, understanding how they reflect the value of nurturing and caring for ourselves and those around us. Michelle Obama's contribution exemplifies how food can be a vehicle for positive change and unity.

Lemon Olive Oil Cake by Meghan, The Duchess of Sussex

Another exquisite recipe gracing this week's activities is the Lemon Olive Oil Cake by Meghan, The Duchess of Sussex. This cake is not merely a dessert; it's a symbol of elegance and simplicity, echoing Meghan's commitment to timeless and meaningful experiences.

71

Through detailed instructions and personal anecdotes, you'll learn how to create this delightful cake and appreciate the joy it can bring. Meghan's recipe represents the idea that food transcends cultural and social boundaries, uniting us in shared moments of delight and connection.

Contributions from Marcus Samuelsson, Ayesha Curry, and More

In this section, you'll have the privilege of exploring contributions from culinary legends such as Marcus Samuelsson and Ayesha Curry, among others. These celebrated chefs and food enthusiasts have lent their talents to the cookbook, offering a diverse array of recipes that showcase their culinary expertise and passion for making a difference.

As you explore these recipes, you'll gain insight into the

unique flavors and cultural influences that have shaped these renowned chefs' careers. Their contributions not only add richness to the cookbook but also highlight the global community that stands behind WCK's mission.

The Impact of Supporting WCK's Emergency Response Efforts

In the concluding pages of this week, we'll delve into the profound impact of supporting

World Central Kitchen's emergency response efforts. You'll witness the tangible results of celebrity support, volunteer efforts, and community collaboration in action.

From providing meals to disaster-stricken areas to fostering lasting change in underserved communities, the impact of WCK's work goes far beyond the kitchen. It's a testament to the enduring belief that by building longer tables instead of higher walls, we can create a world where no one goes hungry.

By the end of this week, you'll not only appreciate the diverse contributions of famous WCK supporters but also recognize the ripple effect of their involvement, inspiring change and hope in countless lives.

1. EXERCISES

Cooking with a Cause: Select

one of the celebrity-contributed recipes introduced this week and prepare it in your own kitchen. Share the experience with friends or family and discuss the impact of celebrity support for WCK.

2. **Supporting WCK**: Research ways to support World Central Kitchen's emergency response efforts in your region or globally. Explore opportunities for fundraising,

volunteering, or raising awareness.

3. **Culinary Exploration**: Choose a recipe from this week's celebrity contributions that is outside your comfort zone or incorporates flavors you've never tried before. Challenge yourself to experiment and expand your culinary horizons.

4. **Community Cookbook**: Organize a community cookbook project where you collect recipes from friends,

family, or local chefs. Consider donating the proceeds to a charitable organization that supports hunger relief.

5. **Celebrity Charity Event**: Plan or participate in a charity event inspired by the contributions of famous supporters of WCK. Whether it's a cooking class, fundraiser, or awareness campaign, channel the enthusiasm and spirit of celebrity support.

QUESTIONS

1. How do celebrity contributions to WCK's cookbook reflect their commitment to humanitarian efforts and food as a force for good?

2. What role do famous supporters play in raising awareness and resources for WCK's mission, and how does this impact the organization's work?

3. Reflecting on the Breakfast Tacos by Michelle Obama, what messages or values do you think celebrities aim to convey through their recipes?

4. How can the diverse array of recipes from renowned chefs inspire individuals to explore new culinary horizons and embrace different flavors and cultures?

5. What inspires you most about the global community that stands behind WCK's mission and supports its emergency

response   efforts?

ACTION PLANS

1. **Cooking for a Cause**: Commit to regularly preparing meals from the WCK cookbook, especially recipes contributed by famous supporters. Share these meals with friends, family, or neighbors, and raise awareness about WCK's mission.

2. **Celebrity Support Campaign**: Launch a campaign or event

that celebrates the contributions of famous supporters of WCK. Raise funds or awareness for the organization's work through this initiative.

3. **Recipe Exchange**: Organize a recipe exchange within your community or workplace. Encourage participants to share their favorite recipes, fostering a sense of connection and unity.

4. **Global Flavors Exploration**: Explore international cuisine

by choosing a recipe from this week's celebrity contributions that represents a different culture or flavor profile. Embrace the opportunity to learn about and appreciate diversity through food.

5. **Supporting Local Initiatives**: Research and get involved with local organizations or initiatives that align with WCK's mission of providing food relief to those in need. Make a plan to volunteer or

contribute resources to these causes.

AFFIRMATIONS

1. I believe in the power of celebrity support to raise awareness and resources for hunger relief, and I am inspired to contribute to this cause.

2. I recognize that food has the ability to transcend boundaries and bring people

together, just as it does in the
WCK cookbook.

3. I am inspired by the diverse
   contributions of famous
   supporters and their
   commitment to making a
   positive impact through food.

4. I acknowledge the far-
   reaching impact of supporting
   WCK's emergency response
   efforts and the lasting change
   it fosters in communities
   worldwide.

5. I am part of a global
   community that understands

the importance of using our resources and talents to build a world where no one goes hungry.

CONCLUSION

As we conclude this journey through "The World Central Kitchen Cookbook" workbook, we invite you to reflect on the profound impact that food can have on our lives and the lives of those less fortunate. Through the exploration of values such as

Urgency, Hope, and Nurturing, you've witnessed how a simple meal can carry with it the power to heal, unite, and inspire change.

You've delved into the heart of humanitarian efforts and seen how World Central Kitchen's tireless dedication to feeding humanity and feeding hope has touched the lives of countless individuals and communities worldwide. You've explored recipes that transcend the realm of mere sustenance, becoming symbols of resilience, unity, and love.

As you move forward from this workbook, remember that you are now part of a global community that understands the importance of building longer tables instead of higher walls. Food, with its ability to nourish both body and soul, becomes a bridge that connects us all. You have the knowledge, the tools, and the inspiration to make a difference, whether in your own kitchen, your local community, or on a broader scale.

World Central Kitchen's mission continues, and so does yours. You carry with you the stories, values, and recipes that have touched your heart and soul. You are equipped to spread the message of hope, compassion, and the transformative power of food. Together, we can create a world where no one goes hungry, where humanity's capacity for generosity knows no bounds.

So, as you turn the final page of this workbook, know that the journey is far from over. It's a journey that takes place every day, in kitchens around the world, in communities coming together to share a meal, and in the hearts of individuals inspired to make a positive impact. Thank you for joining us on this remarkable adventure. Your story, your actions, and your passion contribute to a world filled with nourishment, hope, and humanity.

NOTES

_____

___

_____

___

_____

___

_____

___

_____

___

_____

___

_____

___

_____

___

_____

___

_____

___

_____

___

_____

___

_____

___

____

____

____

____

____

____

_____

___

_____

___

_____

___

_____

___

_____

___

_____

___

_____

___

_____

___

_____

___

_____

___

_____

___

_____

___

_____

___

_____

___

_____

___

_____

___

_____

___

_____

___

_____

—

_____

—

_____

—

_____

—

_____

—

_____

—

_____

___

_____

___

_____

___

_____

___

_____

___

_____

___

_____

___

_____

___

_____

___

_____

___

_____

___

_____

___

_____

___

_____

___

_____

___

_____

___

_____

___

_____

___

_____

___

_____

___

_____

___

_____

___

_____

___

_____

___

_____

___

_____

___

_____

___

_____

___

_____

___

_____

___

_____

___

_____

___

_____

___

_____

___

_____

___

_____

___

_____

__

_____

__

_____

__

_____

__

_____

__

_____

__

_____

___

_____

___

_____

___

_____

___

_____

___

_____

___

_____

___

_____

___

_____

___

_____

___

_____

___

_____

___

_____

___

_____

___

_____

___

_____

___

_____

___

_____

___

———————————————————————

——

———————————————————————

——

———————————————————————

——

———————————————————————

——

———————————————————————

——

———————————————————————

——

_____

___

_____

___

_____

___

_____

___

_____

___

_____

___

_____

___

_____

___

_____

___

_____

___

_____

___

_____

___

_____

___

_____

___

_____

___

_____

___

_____

___

_____

___

146

_____

___

_____

___

_____

___

_____

___

_____

___

_____

___

_____

___

_____

___

_____

___

_____

___

_____

___

_____

___

_____

___

_____

___

_____

___

Made in United States
Troutdale, OR
04/06/2024